THE DRESDEN FRAUENKIRCHE

Published by the
Dresden Frauenkirche Foundation

Translated by Alan Lloyd Nothnagle
(in cooperation with Patricia Ruka-Ahr)

EVANGELISCHE VERLAGSANSTALT
Leipzig

Picture Credits:
SLUB/Dt. Fotothek: picture. 2, 3, 4, 9
IPRO Dresden Planungs- und Ingenieuraktiengesellschaft: picture 15, 16
Stadtarchiv Dresden, Sammlung Risse (17.1.2) R. 18 Nr. 30: picture 7
Jürgen Rach: picture 10
Oliver Killig: picture 59
Rene Gaens: picture 57
Frauke Thielking: picture 58
Staatl. Kunstsammlungen Dresden: picture 5, 6
Jörg Schöner, Dresden: all the other pictures

Bibliographic information published by the Deutsche Nationalbibliothek
The Deutsche Nationalbibliothek lists this publication in the Deutsche Nationalbibliographie; detailed
bibliographic data are available on the Internet at http://dnb.dnb.de.

3., rev. a. upd. Edition 2016
© 2005 by Evangelische Verlagsanstalt GmbH, Leipzig
Printed in Germany

Design and layout: makena plangrafik GbR, Leipzig
Printing and binding: Grafisches Centrum Cuno, Calbe

ISBN 978-3-374-04759-8

www.eva-leipzig.de
www.frauenkirche-dresden.de

TABLE OF CONTENTS

1 The rebuilt Frauenkirche.

THE CHURCH AND ITS CONSTRUCTION HISTORY

PREVIOUS CHURCH

For over 1000 years the site upon which the modern-day Frauenkirche is located has been a place of prayer and meeting for the congregation. Here stood Dresden's earliest church. It was consecrated to Mary, the mother of Jesus thus the name »To Our Beloved Lady«, from which today's »Frauenkirche« is derived. It began as a so-called »original parish«, used as a base for missionary work among the surrounding Slavic settlements. Twenty-six parishes were centred here. After the Reformation was introduced to Dresden on 6 July 1539, the Frauenkirche became an Evangelical-Lutheran church. However, by the dawning of the 18th century the earlier Gothic church was in a woeful state. Thus, with the consent of King August the Strong, the Dresden city council decided to demolish the old church and construct a new one. August, the Prince Elector of Saxony had long wanted to redesign the city around the site of the old Frauenkirche. He was particularly unhappy with the location of the church's cemetery in the centre of his capital.

THE 18TH CENTURY CHURCH

In 1722, the city of Dresden commissioned George Bähr, the council's master carpenter, to plan the new house of God. However, construction was delayed. The plans were changed several times before the cornerstone was finally laid on 26 August 1726. Construction lasted a total of seventeen years. The building cost 288,000 Saxonian Talers, a sum which was largely provided by the Dresden citizenry.

The basic structure of the Frauenkirche was consecrated in 1734. While the inner dome was complete, there was neither a main dome nor an altar and organ. The Dresden superintendent Valentin Ernst Löscher pressured his

2 The previous church »To Our Beloved Lady«, view from the south, copper engraving by Moritz Bodenehr, 1714.

builders to complete the Frauenkirche and open it for worship. This decision was a reaction to the tension which had been growing between the Catholic court and the Lutheran citizenry. The Saxonian Prince Elector August the Strong had converted to the Catholic faith in 1697 in order to assume the crown of Poland – a highly unpopular step in one of the core regions of the Reformation. He had promised his subjects that they would be allowed to continue to live their Lutheran faith without interference. Nevertheless, the Church and the town's citizenry feared the Catholic prince's expansionist efforts,

and intended the early consecration as an open sign of defiance.

The installation of the tower cross in 1743 marked the end of construction. George Bähr had died five years previously. Nevertheless, he lived long enough to witness the completion of the unconventional main dome. It is regarded as his masterpiece: he had transformed a carpenter's model into a monumental but seemingly weightless stone dome, comparable to those of St. Peter in Rome and the Duomo in Florence. The plan for this central dome above a quadratic ground plan with bevelled corners developed over a multi-year process which also involved State Architect Johann Christoph Knöffel. But the decision to build this unique 12,000 t, bell-shaped stone dome, also called »the stone bell«, was made by George Bähr alone. It is this »bell« which has made the Frauenkirche the most celebrated stone-domed building north of the Alps. The original plan had called for a wooden construction sheathed in copper, but rising copper prices made this idea impossible. This gave George Bähr the opportunity to push through his own idea of a stone dome – sandstone was abundantly available in local quarries.

However, this dome was highly controversial: the first cracks appeared shortly after its completion, although before the construction of the lantern. They were caused by the visibly too narrow foundations of the internal columns, which sank into the ground more quickly than the external walls and thus led to different settling processes throughout the building. Since George Bähr was no longer alive, the concerned city council commissioned renowned architects, including Gaetano Chiaveri, the architect of the Hofkirche, to examine the situation and prepare reports.

3 View from the Neustädter bank upon the silhouette of the Old Town, about 1930.

4 George Bähr's Frauenkirche, about 1930,
photo: Walter Möbius.

5 Bernardo Belotto (Canaletto): The Neumarkt
of Dresden, view from the Moritzstraße, about
1750. State Art Collections Dresden, Old Masters
Picture Gallery.

Chiaveri recommended dismantling the heavy stone dome and replacing it with a wooden dome. However, the council did not follow his suggestion, which was the result of imprecise examination. The cracks were sealed and the stone dome held for centuries. Nevertheless, new cracks continued to appear, which is why construction work on the dome is visible in the paintings of Bernardo Bellotto (Canaletto).

Today, building specialists cannot hide their admiration for the achievement of their forebears, who succeeded in constructing this celebrated church without the benefit of modern static calculations and the tools of modern technology.

The dome of the Frauenkirche underwent a crucial test during the Seven Years War. In 1760 Dresden was laid siege to by Prussian troops and taken

under cannon fire. Many of the town's buildings – such as the Kreuzkirche – succumbed to the onslaught. But the cannon balls bounced off the stone dome of the Frauenkirche, inspiring Prussian King Frederick II to say to his artillery commander: »Let the fat head stand.« From this event arose the legend that the Church was indestructible.

The church's nave has a relatively small ground plan of 45 by 45 metres.

The interior owes its monumental aspect to its height. The central internal dome rises 37 meters. Through its circa seven metre wide opening, one can look up 68 metres into the main dome. Bright, understated colours and well-conceived lighting effects express the joy of faith and give the interior a festive air. Here the Lutheran faith has been provided with an architectural and artistic expression in even the tiniest of its loving details. The colour scheme grows more radiant the closer one comes to the chancel. The chancel itself is decorated in white and gold, but also shows traces of its fate and incorporates them chromatically. During the reconstruction, the designers undertook great efforts to identify and match the original 1738 colour scheme. Lime and casein colours as well as golf leaf were used.

The interior is oriented on the altar and pulpit. The pulpit's central location in the centre of the sanctuary balustrade is particularly conspicuous. The sermon is held from this point. Its message invites the faithful to receive the Holy Communion in the chancel. Seven large doors of nearly equal size allow visitors to enter and depart. The city council explicitly rejected the representative main entrance favoured by August the Strong. The well-conceived architectural programme expresses the notion that everyone is to feel welcome in the Frauenkirche without respect of persons. The placing of the seven doors also expresses the desire to carry the message of this unique house of God to all points of the compass.

Eight slender columns, arranged in a circle, shape the interior and share the immense weight of the dome. They are linked to the external walls through shear walls. Thus the main dome's weight is partially distributed to the external walls. The internal dome rises above the centre, which – with its five semicircular galleries – is oriented on the altar and pulpit. The prayer booths in the lowest gallery, which could be purchased in George

6 Bernardo Belotto (Canaletto): The Neumarkt of Dresden, view from the Jüdenhof, about 1749, State Art Collections Dresden, Old Masters Picture Gallery.

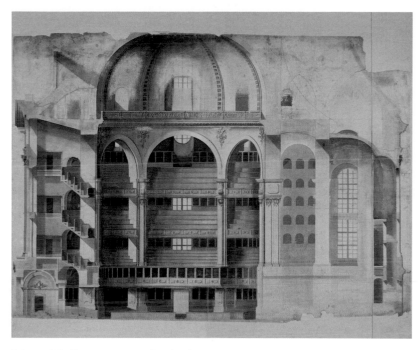

7 George Bähr: The Frauenkirche of Dresden, third sketch, 1726, longitudinal section with galleries.

Bährs Frauenkirche, are provided with windows. One intention underlying the construction of the baroque Frauenkirche was to bring together as many people as possible within a limited space. The builders thought nothing of creating approximately 3,200 seats (around 1,800 today) without a clear view of the altar. They thought it more important that everyone should be able to hear the sermon. In his consecration sermon of 1734, Valentin Ernst Löschner expressly described churches as auditoriums »where people come together to hear God's word and to receive the holy sacraments«.

George Bähr is often quoted as saying that he wanted to build a church which »would be as one stone from the ground upward«. The Frauenkirche's nicknames, »faith transformed into stone« or »the true St. Peter's of the Lutheran religion«, point to the architectural implementation of the Lutheran notion of worship, in which the word of God takes centre stage. As Martin Luther stated in his sermon collection of 1526: »There is no other reason to build churches than for the Christians to come together, to pray, to hear sermons, and to receive the sacraments.«

DESTRUCTION AND RUIN

The legend of the Frauenkirche's indestructibility (cf. p. 9) seemed valid at first during the bombing attack of 13 February 1945. When the Second World War, which Germany unleashed, fell back upon Dresden, and Allied bombers destroyed 15 km² of the central city, the Frauenkirche – the city's symbol – remained standing. While a firestorm raged in the central city, the crypt provided shelter for some 300 people.

This time, too, the bombs bounced off the stone dome. However, the fire penetrated the shattered windows, spread to the interior, and destroyed all the wooden structures and furnishings.

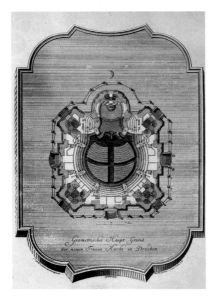

8 Ground plan after George Bähr's projection, drawn by Johann Georg Schmidt, engraved by Christian Philipp Lindemann, 1736.

A temperature of over 1000 ° Celsius developed. On the morning of 15 February, 1945, towards 10 AM, the gutted dome collapsed – first with a light crackling noise, and then with a deafening crash.

For forty-five years the ruin of the Frauenkirche lay like an open wound in the heart of the city. The leaders of the GDR lacked not only the money but also the will to rebuild it. Nevertheless, the Frauenkirche stayed alive in the hearts of many Dresden citizens. In 1966 the city council classified the ruin as a memorial. Each year, state representatives laid wreaths on the anniversary of the bombing.

In the 1980s the church peace movement developed another form of commemoration. Following the ecumenical »Peace Forum« in the Kreuzkirche on the evening of 13 February 1982, young people marched to the ruin of the Frauenkirche. The candles which they carried in remembrance of the horrors of war and as a protest against the militarisation of their country marked the beginning of a new kind of commemoration. This impressive act was also an example of people displaying the courage of their convictions in the face of state repression.

RECONSTRUCTION

As early as 1988, prominent West German politicians began calling for the reconstruction of the Frauenkirche. At the time of the »Wende« in 1989, a citizen's group formed in Dresden for the purpose of rebuilding the Frauenkirche. On

9 Ruin of the Frauenkirche with the fallen Luther monument, photo. Richard Peter sen.

10 Commemoration at the ruin.

13 February 1990, a call went out from Dresden to the world requesting help in rebuilding the Frauenkirche. This appeal attracted a wide response. The »Society for the Promotion of the Rebuilding of the Dresden Frauenkirche« chaired by the musician Ludwig Güttler was formed and focused the immense outpouring of voluntary work on the part of many people.

In 1994 the Evangelical-Lutheran State Church of Saxony, the Free State of Saxony, and the city of Dresden created the Dresden Frauenkirche Foundation. It assumed the building supervision and the responsibility for the reconstructed church. More than 100,000 private donors have helped make the reconstruction of the Frauenkirche possible. These include the Society to Promote the Reconstruction of the Frauenkirche as well as the twenty-five friends' groups at home and abroad with their 13,000 members, along with the Dresdner Bank and the ZDF television network.

The first step in the rebuilding process occurred in 1993. An elaborate archaeological rubble clearing programme made it possible to reuse large portions of the original structure. Reconstruction proper began with the laying of the first stone in May 1994 under the guidance of building director Eberhard Burger. It essentially followed three main ideas: George Bähr's Frauenkirche should be reconstructed (1) with as much of the original building material as possible according to the original plans, (2) with the use of modern technology and modern knowledge of structural analysis and construction physics, and (3) with attention to the requirements for a constructive use of the building in the 21st century.

The external reconstruction of the Frauenkirche was completed after ten years of work on 22 June 2004, with the installation of the cupola and the gilded tower cross. After the completion of internal construction, the Frauenkirche was consecrated on 30 October 2005, in an atmosphere of joy and thankfulness.

The considerable reuse of the historical fabric has made the war's destructive force visible in the »new Frauenkirche«. The dark coloration of the old stones which were salvaged during the archaeological rubble clearing, then measured, photographed, inventoried, and tested for stability, is reminiscent of the scars of a healed wound.

After some eighty years of wind and weather, the light-coloured new stones will also have taken on the dark grey patina typical of sandstone. Nevertheless, the different dimensions of the old construction segments, the crack in the eastern choir annex, and the gaps in the capitals will remain visible as »scars of the healed wound«. Thus the Frauenkirche will continue to give testimony to the history of its destruction. But at the same time it is also a testimony to the overcoming of enmity and a symbol of hope and reconciliation. The reconstruction principle of »building bridges – living reconciliation – strengthening faith« will retain its power and timeliness long after the consecration will have become just a distant memory.

11 Archaeological rubble clearing, September 1993.

12 Building with scaffolding and shed roof, May 2002.

13 Laying of the first stone on 27 May 1994.

14 Dimensional variation in the connected areas, interlocking of the stair tower E with the west side window, Oktober 1999.

15 Plan of the ground floor.

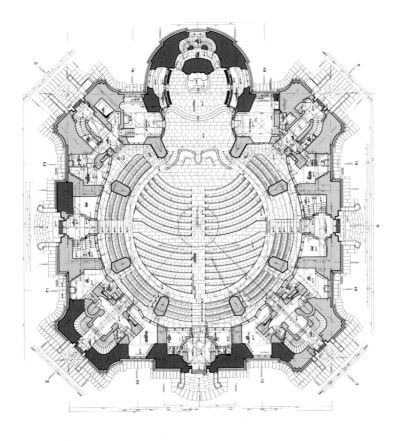

17 Sanctuary.

INTERIOR

SANCTUARY WITH ALTAR AND ORGAN

The sanctuary with its altar and organ case begins behind the sanctuary balustrade. During the reconstruction, the planners wondered whether the balustrade might not be in the way. Nevertheless, they decided to reconstruct the balustrade since it is essential to the space's architectural and artistic assembly and also represents an important component of the overall spatial programme of liturgy and worship. Unlike most pre-Reformation churches, the space behind the sanctuary balustrade is not reserved to clergy. Instead, everyone is invited to enter the special area of the sanctuary to receive Holy Communion or to be baptised. Weddings are performed here as well.

For acoustic reasons it was formerly difficult to understand the minister in all areas of the Frauenkirche. That is why in 1739, shortly after Bähr's death, a decision was made to construct a new and richly decorated covered pulpit on the left sanctuary column. This later pulpit was not included in the reconstruction because of the availability of modern sound amplification technology. Thus the pulpit in the centre of the sanctuary area has reassumed its role as the centre of annunciation, as George Bähr originally intended it.

The church's interior is oriented on the altar and organ. The sandstone altar of 1738, fashioned by sculptor Johann Christian Feige according to a design by George Bähr, is dominated by a scene of »Jesus on the Mount of Olives«.

During the archaeological rubble clearing, the architects were surprised and delighted to discover that large portions of the altar were largely intact: the altar table, the columns with their capitals, and portions of the background emerged from the debris. Some 2,000 fragments of the destroyed altar were salvaged and identified. Through painstaking work, the individual fragments were categorised and inserted into the archaeological reconstruction. The salvaged pieces were sketched, examined in regard to their coloration, and categorised by the restorers.

18 Detail of the altar: Jesus with the annunciating angel.

Nearly 80% of the original sandstone sculptures have been preserved. Missing portions were complemented with special cement additions. Plaster and wooden ornaments, such as the angels above the praying Christ and the gloriole, were created anew. The altar's colour scheme was designed to highlight the original message. However, attentive observers will also recognise traces of the tragic fate which the altar shared with the entire church.

The altar table also holds a place for the Cross of Nails. It is a symbol of the reconciliation work which began after the war in the cathedral of the Midlands town of Coventry, which was destroyed by German bombers in 1940. Today, the Frauenkirche is linked with over 160 reconciliation centres world-wide in the International Community of the Cross of Nails. In its efforts to spread peace and reconciliation, this movement has taken upon itself the legacy of history and the message of Jesus.

During the original construction of the Frauenkirche, a fierce debate raged over the design of the altar. Other themes had been planned originally: earlier designs envisioned the birth of Christ, the sacrifice of Isaac, or the resurrected Christ. However, in December 1733 the Dresden City Council came out strongly favour of the scene on the Mount of Olives. In the night before Good Friday, in the hour of his greatest

19 Detail of the altar: The sleeping disciples.

20 Cross of Nails on the altar table.

isolation and danger, Jesus kneels down to pray in the Garden of Gethsemane. His disciples have fallen asleep, and already we can see the approach of the soldiers – led by Judas – who will take him prisoner.

But the sandstone altar sculpture does not only quote the Passion story but also presents the story of Jesus's suffering in all its consequences. By drawing the observer's eye upward from the praying Jesus, the image points to the basic Christian idea underlying Jesus's passion: the suffering of Jesus links humankind to God. The upward-pointing movement of the praying Christ leads to the angel, who offers him strength and clarity for the path of suffering which lies before him. Above this image we see angels bearing the cross, the symbol of devotion and suffering, to where the gloriole symbolises the glory of God. Golden beams emerge from the wreath of clouds in the centre of which the eye of God in an equilateral triangle represents the presence of the Trinitarian God and his compassionate faithfulness.

Garlands of wheat and grapes extend from the gloriole to the right and left. They represent the bread and wine, gifts of God at communion. Distributed to each individual with the words »given for you« and »shed for you«, they link us to the loving kindness and forgiveness of God. Just as bread and wine are given out to the congregation, so too has Christ given himself for the peace of the world.

On each side of the central altar scene we find figures from the Old and New Testament. Moses, the prophet who led the people of Israel from their Egyptian bondage, sits on the outer left edge. He is depicted with the two tablets containing the Ten Commandments. He holds up the so-called »first tablet« with the three commandments relating to God. These commandments, which are the basis for faith, hope, and love, provide the foundation for the commandments of the »second tablet«, which

protect humankind's social existence. On the outer right edge we see Aaron. His robe, turban, breastplate, and censer identify him as a representative of the Old Testament priesthood. He served as one of Moses's closest collaborators in the tabernacle. Together they represent God's covenant with his people of Israel and recall the tasks given to all Christians to admonish others as prophets and comfort them as priests.

The two upright New Testament apostle figures of Paul and Philipp flank the central scene. They represent the Annunciation which refers to the life of Christ. The books they hold in their hands point to this. Paul's sword symbolises the clarity and precision of the divine Word while also indicating the assumed manner of his death. Philipp's cross staff symbolises the spread of faith through Christian missionary activity. Both are depicted in such a way as if they were »hearing« their message from the events in the centre of the

21 Communion chalices, 1705, 1793, 1598 (from the left).

22 Detail of the altar: Moses and Paul.

23 Detail of the altar: Philipp and Aaron.

image. After all, they are proclaiming nothing other than the message of the gospels of Jesus Christ.

The figures form a harmonious whole. They appear animate and full of atmosphere and tension. The dynamic movements of their gestures and clothing are typical for baroque sculpture. The ensemble of figures turns to the observer and seems to come alive.

Above the altar table one can see a dedicatory plaque displaying three relief figures: Love (with the heart), Faith (with the cross), and Hope (with the anchor). They repeat the theme from

the inner dome and surround the dedicatory text »Christo deprecatori, fidem spondet, amorem declarat, spem consecrat omnia illi debens. Se Pop. Q. Dresdensis« – »To Christ, the intermediary, the council and people of Dresden proclaim the conviction of their faith, declare love, dedicate hope, and give all thanks.«

The organ stands majestically above the altar. It assumes a central role in Lutheran worship services. Today, as before, the proclamation of the Christian faith unfolds in the unity of word, music, and

24 Detail of the altar: Angel with ears.

the sharing of the sacraments. Church music serves the honour of God. This is attested to in the three letters in the lozenge above the organ: S.D.G. – *Soli Deo Gloria* (To God Alone the Glory). George Bähr designed the altar and the organ case as a unit. The visible part of the organ, facing the church interior, was reconstructed accordingly.

The original organ of the Dresden Frauenkirche was one of a total of four major creations of the great Saxonian organ builder, Gottfried Silbermann. It was dedicated in 1736. Shortly after its completion, it was also tested by Johann Sebastian Bach. In order to adapt the instrument to changing musical demands, it underwent numerous changes in the 18th and 19th centuries and was thoroughly rebuilt and expanded in the 20th century. Recordings from the years preceding the Second World War with the Frauenkirche's organist Hans Ander-Donath at the keys give us an impression of the sound produced by this altered instrument.

The Frauenkirche's new organ maintains a close relationship to the one built by Gottfried Silbermann, even though it does not claim to reproduce

25 The new organ of the Frauenkirche, made by the Strasbourg organ builder Daniel Kern.

either the earlier sound or the old technology. The result was an instrument which pays tribute to the organ's history while fulfilling the demands of modern organ construction and modern musical practice. The organ-building workshop of Daniel Kern in Strasbourg, which is closely involved with the work of Andreas Silbermann, the brother and teacher of Gottfried Silbermann, constructed the organ. The organ case was fashioned by highly qualified cabinet makers and wood sculptors.

In order to do justice to the music of both the period of the Frauenkirche's construction and also music from the 19th and 20th centuries, the claviature ranges were designed accordingly and extend from the large »C« to a three-point »a« in the manuals and to a one point »g« in the pedals. In addition to the three baroque systems, the arrangement has four manuals, 67 registers, and 4,790 pipes. In order to assist the organist in preparing concerts, the organ contains an electronic composition device whereby combinations of registers can be stored. The brustwerk can be tuned from today's modern chamber tone to the baroque tone, which is one half tone lower.

INNER DOME

At a height of 26 metres, the central inner dome rises above the church's interior. Their arches pick up the rhythmic design of the inner columns and lead them up to the capitals beneath the circular eye of the inner dome, which provides us with a view far beyond into the main

26 The organ in detail.

dome of the church. The inner dome is divided into eight pictorial sections. The four large panels in the light-guiding main axes depict the four Evangelists Matthew, Mark, Luke, and John. The four smaller pictorial sections show allegories of the Christian virtues of Faith, Hope, and Love. Mercy is also shown.

The original painting was undertaken between May and November 1734 by the Venetian artist Johann Battista Grone, who, as a painter at the Dresden court, had previously created numerous much admired theatre designs and ceiling paintings in the homes of prominent

27 Inner Dome.

28 Evangelist Matthew.

29 Allegory of Love.

Dresden citizens. The modern painting of the inner dome was carried out by the Dresden painter Christoph Wetzel who learned to imitate Johann Battista Grone's painting style after long and intensive studies.

In keeping with a tradition extending back to the church fathers Hieronymus and Gregory the Great, the four Evangelists, as witnesses of the life of Jesus, are each attributed with a characteristic symbol. Matthew is linked to a quasi-human being, since his gospel begins with Jesus's human descent. Markus is shown with a lion, since the sermon of John in the desert stands at the beginning of his gospel. The gospel of Luke begins with the altar sacrifice of

the priest Zacharias, which is why he is depicted with a bull, a sacrificial animal. Finally, John is accompanied by an eagle, because his gospel is concerned with the elevation of Jesus.

The mastery in depiction demonstrates itself in the individual characterisation of the Evangelists. The angel attributed to Matthew points to a piece of writing lying before him. This is probably a reference to the numerous Old Testament quotations which link the Gospel of Matthew to the Hebrew Bible. Mark listens to the roar of the lion, which the Old Testament prophets had compared to the mighty word of God. Luke, who claimed that his own work was based on eyewitness reports, looks

30 Allegory of Mercy.

31 Evangelist Mark.

meditatively into an open book. By contrast, John, whose gospel is considered to be the most »spiritual«, is depicted with his eyes looking upward at the moment of inspiration.

The allegories of the three celebrated Christian virtues of Faith, Hope, and Love are depicted in the usual iconographical manner. Faith stands as a woman gazing at the cross in her right hand. In addition, she holds a communion chalice in her left hand. The female figure of Hope extends her arm out toward a beam of light coming from above, and is characterised by an anchor, since hope in Jesus has a secure foundation. Love holds a flaming heart in her hand. The children assembled

around her symbolise the whole of love-hungry humanity. It is no accident that these three virtues are complemented by Mercy, depicted as a woman dropping coins into the hat of a needy person. Then and now, Mercy refers to those persons who, on account of social problems, have need of our help and support.

Beneath the dome panels of the four Evangelists, and above the virtues, we see medallions with biblical scenes. These are artistic designs from our own times. The eight original panels were most likely filled with similar relief images. Since there was no information on the original content, a new pictorial programme was designed in

32 Evangelist John.

33 Allegory of Faith.

direct reference to the existing paintings on the inner dome. The oval panels above the four virtues were arranged according to the parables of Jesus from the New Testament. It was in such expressive parables that Jesus brought his message to life for ordinary people. The parables were selected to match the virtues with which they have been juxtaposed. For example, the parable of the »asking friend« (Luke 11:5–13) is located above the figure of Faith (»fides«), for in this parable Jesus encourages us to pray faithfully. Above the virtue of Mercy (»misericordia«) is the parable of the »Good Samaritan« (Luke 10:30–35). With this parable, Jesus encouraged his listeners to recognise the needy »Other«

as one's neighbour and to offer him help. In the oval panel above Love (»caritas«) we see the parable of the Prodigal Son (Luke 15:11–24). In this parable, Jesus presents God as the loving father who abandons no one. Above Hope (»spe«) is depicted the parable of »the Sower« (Luke 8:4–8), showing how after much lost effort seeds eventually sprout and yield hundredfold.

With the Four Evangelists, the oval panels are located under the large-scale figures. Since Matthew, Mark, Luke, and John related the message of the life and work of Jesus, it made sense to juxtapose central deeds from their respective gospels. Thus, under the figure of John we find the healing

34 Allegory of Hope.

35 Evangelist Luke.

of a sick person (John 5:1–14) and under the figure of the Evangelist Mark
we find the scene of the blessing of
the children (Mark 10 13–16). Under
the Evangelist Matthew we see Jesus
as a teacher during the Sermon on the
Mount (Matthew 5:9), while beneath
the Evangelist Luke we see the calling
of Peter (Luke 5:1–11). The combina-
tion of all four scenes depicts Jesus
healing, blessing, teaching, and calling
on others to follow his example.

THE TOWER CROSS

The Frauenkirche's old tower cross has
its place on the south side of the church's
interior. When the Frauenkirche collapsed on the morning of 15 February

1945, it fell from a height of 92 metres
and lay for decades beneath the rubble.
The joy and gratitude were immense
when it was salvaged during the archaeological rubble clearing in 1993 – de-
formed but not destroyed.

Its placement in the church's interior is intended as a permanent admo-
nition. Visitors are invited to record a
prayer request for peace and reconciliation in the book and light a candle
alongside the cross.

Today a copy of the original tower
cross crowns the Frauenkirche – a gift
from the British people, organised by
the sponsoring group »Dresden Trust«.
The new tower cross was presented
to the Frauenkirche Foundation on

36 Medaillon: Parable of the sower. **37** Medaillon: Parable of the Good Samaritan.

13 February 2000, the fifty-fifth anniversary of the Dresden bombing. It is now visible for miles around as an impressive symbol of friendship and reconciliation.

38 The old tower cross.

39 The new tower cross, erected on the building site of the Frauenkirche, August 2002.

40 Salvaging the old tower cross on June 1, 1993.

41 Bell in the bellcage.

BELLS

The bells of the Frauenkirche are not visible to the eye, but are clearly audible throughout the city. They ring out the hours and call the faithful to worship services, devotion, and prayer. Seven new bells were forged in December 2002 and April 2003 in Bad Friedrichshall and Karlsruhe. Together with an old bell from the year 1518, they make up the chimes of the Frauenkirche. The Frauenkirche's new bells represent the fifth set over the church's long and turbulent history. Before its destruction, it had only four bells which were all located in the south-west stair tower and were larger than the new bells. But the bell environment around the Frauenkirche has also changed in the intervening years. Thus it was necessary to plan chimes which would harmonise with the bells of the nearby Kreuzkirche and Cathedral.

Today, the bells have been distributed among the two western stair towers and have been attached to free-standing oaken bell cages. This helps prevent the damage which the bells' vibrations formerly caused to the masonry.

At the beginning of the modern era it was customary to supply bells both with a name and a biblical inscription and an artistic design. The chimes' designers decided to revive this old, nearly forgotten tradition. Each of the bells has been given a biblical name which also makes a statement about its character and function. Thus the largest among them bears the name of the prophet Isaiah and the bible verse from the book of the same name: »And they shall beat their swords into ploughshares« (Isaiah 2:4). As a peace bell, it assumes one of the Frauenkirche's most important duties. Each day at noon it calls people to reflection and to prayers for peace. The oldest of the Frauenkirche's bells has also been integrated into the set of seven new bells.

It bears the name Maria. Cast in 1518, it originally formed part of the chimes of the Altzella monastery near Nossen. Following the closing of the monastery, it was installed in the original medieval Frauenkirche. While its sister bells were melted down for military purposes during the First World War, it escaped this sad fate. When the chimes were renewed in 1925, it was removed since its tone did not match the new chimes. Hanging in the Wermsdorf church, it was thus the only one of the Frauenkirche's bells to survive the Second World War and later ended up in the village church of Dittmansdorf.

42 Jesaja.

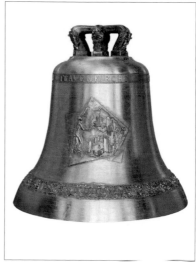

43 Johannes.

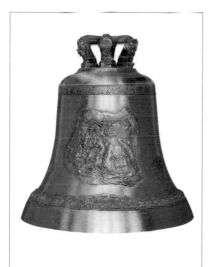

44 Jeremia.

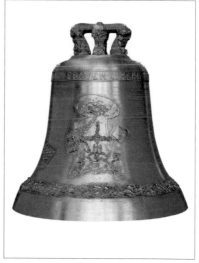

45 Josua.

46 Maria.

47 David.

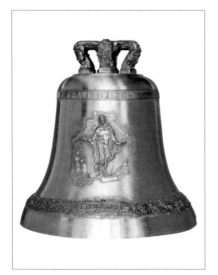

48 Philippus.

49 Hanna.

42

Bell	»Jesaja«, Peace Bell.

Name:	Jesaja
Saying:	»And they shall beat their swords into ploughshares« (Isaiah 2:4)
Function:	Peace Bell
Nominal.	d'+2
Lower:	1390 mm
Mass:	1600 kg

43

Bell	»John«, Annunciation Bell.

Name:	John
Saying:	»Prepare ye the way of the Lord« (Matthew 3:3)
Function:	Annunciation Bell
Nominal:	e'+3
Lower	1230 mm
Mass:	1100 kg

44

Bell	»Jeremia«, City Bell.

Name:	Jeremia
Saying:	»And seek the peace of the city!« (Jeremiah 29.7)
Function:	City Bell
Nominal:	g'+3
Lower:	1000 mm
Mass:	820 kg

45

Bell	»Josua«, Wedding Bell.

Name:	Josua
Saying:	»As for me and my house, we will serve the Lord« (Joshua 24.15)
Function:	Wedding Bell
Nominal:	a'+3
Lower:	950 mm
Mass:	570 kg

46

Bell	»Maria«, Memorial Bell.

Name:	Maria
Saying:	afe maria gracia plena dominus thekum mader myseri kortie Mccccc xviii jar
Function:	Memorial Bell
Nominal:	b'-5.5
Lower:	846 mm
Mass:	380 kg

47

Bell	»David«, Prayer Bell.

Name:	David
Saying:	»Hear me when I call« (Psalm 4:1)
Function:	Prayer Bell
Nominal:	c"+4
Lower:	850 mm
Mass:	420 kg

48

Bell	»Philipp«, Baptismal Bell.

Name:	Philipp
Saying:	»One Lord, one faith, one baptism« (Ephesians 4:5)
Function:	Baptismal Bell
Nominal:	d"+4
Lower:	780 mm
Mass:	330 kg

49

Bell	»Hanna«, Bell of Thanks.

Name:	Hanna
Saying:	»My heart rejoiceth in the Lord« (I. Samuel 2:1)
Function:	Bell of Thanks
Nominal:	f"+5
Lower:	680 mm
Mass:	270 kg

50 Lower Church, southeastern chapel: Room of the Ten Commandments.

LOWER CHURCH

We would now like to invite you to visit the Lower Church. Today it serves as a place of silence. Visitors are requested to respect the special character of this space.

During reconstruction a decision was made to establish a church in the lower area. It was consecrated in 1996. During the reconstruction, numerous worship and prayer services, church tours, concerts, and lectures took place here.

The shape of a Greek cross, which is visible throughout the building, is most obvious here. The four diagonal arms of the cross house four rooms which were used for burial after 1728. The burial chambers replaced the cemetery, which surrounded the previous church and which was disbanded upon the reconstruction of the baroque Frauenkirche. Burial beneath the church meant a symbolic and permanent link between the living and the dead in the »community of saints«. 244 interments occurred in the burial chambers between 1728 and 1787.

During the destruction of the Frauenkirche, only the south-western burial chamber remained undamaged. The individually mortared tombs have remained largely intact. The other burial chambers were revaulted during reconstruction and now serve as prayer chapels.

At the centre of the Lower Church, forming a sort of cornerstone, is a monumental altar stone which the British artist Anish Kapoor fashioned from a slab of heavily marbled Irish limestone. Because of its unusual form, this »stone of contention« provokes visitors to reflect on their lives and the world. Particularly the funnel-like depression in the centre raises questions: does it – as an allusion to ancient sacrificial altars – recall the victims of war and violence? Or is it a reference to the essential definition of depth, which so easily gets lost in the superficiality of everyday life? Particularly notable here is the contrast between the polished surface of the stone and its seemingly unhewn sides.

51 Lower Church, central room.

In the Lower Church too, the Frauenkirche's fate is easily recognisable. The preserved masonry of the vertical walls with its hand-hewn stones flows into the news stones of the vaulted ceiling. The wounds of the bombing are particularly evident in the north-western chapel. The artistic designs of the Berlin sculptor Michael Schoenholtz in the central room and the four ancient tombs poignantly evoke destruction and renewal, wounds and healing, danger and protection, death and life.

The south-west chapel is designed as a prayer and meditation room. Two of the benches on the side walls »frame« a large vertical stone sculpture. The ten blocks with their Roman numerals, from which the sculpture is assembled, symbolise the Ten Commandments. The weight and monumental quality of this »Tower of Commandments« appeal to the ultimate foundation of our humanity. The Ten Commandments of the Hebrew Bible are recognised far beyond the boundaries of the individual denominations as the fundamental principles of human society.

The north-western chapel displays tombstones discovered during the rubble clearing, most of which came from the old churchyard. Some of them were used as building material during the construction of the baroque Frauenkirche and were painstakingly restored and conserved following their salvaging. Thus these tombstones not only recall the remote history of the previous church, but also the original function of the lower rooms as the »new« Frauenkirche's place of burial. With their largely still readable inscriptions and reliefs, they remind us that our earthly existence is fleeting. As stone witnesses to history, they recall earlier generations and their faith legacy. For although they give a drastic depiction of human finiteness in a time when death was accepted as a fact of life, these tombstones also testify to a living hope of resurrection. Michael Schoenholtz picked up on this idea by arranging three fragments of an old stone crucifix into an expressive sculpture. The fragments probably came from a sculpture which was captured on an ancient copperplate engraving of the old Frauenkirche from the middle of the 16th century. Above the passage across from the entrance, they form the clearly visible highlight of the room. They are reminiscent of an angel. Thus the view of the stone evidence of our mortality is transcended, and thus the thoughts of the observer are led beyond the boundaries of death.

The north-western chapel gives the clearest testimony to the war's destructive force. Here, the wounds have remained unhealed and are presented with graphic elements. The window across from the entrance was closed by

52 Lower Church, north-eastern chapel: Room of the tombstones.

53 Lower Church, north-western chapel: Room of destruction.

a design in relief. The broken shape of a cross, which seems to have been broken out of its frame, has been inserted into the floor. Thus disengaged from the total design, this cross serves as a sort of tomb slab. It appears again in the central space in the form of the floating cross which has been reinstalled above the altar.

The tombs in the south-western chapel are largely undamaged and thus were left untouched. This room itself is not accessible, however one can reach the upper part of the chapel through a passage. From here one has an attractive view of the vaults of the lower space. This chapel with its two levels represents one of the few entirely undamaged sections of the church. For this reason the artist decided to provide hope with an artistic design. Two smaller sculptures are arranged on the two clearly visible capitals above the supporting elements of the vault. They symbolise growth and live, representing »hope

beyond the grave«. The sculptures were conceived as a couple and both represent growth. One of them extends horizontally and the other vertically. They associate the terrestrial and celestial realms. The outlines of both sculptures once again recall the shape of a cross.

The choir chapel is located east of the Lower Church. It contains two sculptures in many parts which are placed symbolically facing each other. Both sculptures consists of nearly identical elements. While »Destruction« still gives a hint of the original shape, »Reconstruction« is in a thoroughly incomplete state. The juxtaposition of the two sculptures makes us witnesses of a process in which the progress from destruction to reconstruction cannot be taken for granted. Instead, there is always a danger that a reconstructed edifice can be destroyed once more. This reminds us that we are continually called upon to stand up to the powers of destruction.

54 Lower Church, above the vaults in the southwestern chapel: Niche of hope.

55 / 56 Lower Church, choir chapel:
Room of decision.

51

57 Chamber Choir of the Frauenkirche, conducted by Cantor Matthias Grünert.

AN OPEN HOUSE
OF GOD AND MAN

The Dresden Frauenkirche is an open church for people from near and far. The church interior, the tower, and the Lower Church are all highlights. And yet the Frauenkirche is far more than a mere tourist attraction.

Thanks to the history made manifest in its structure, and through its many offerings, the Frauenkirche is a symbol of peace. It invites us to re-examine our history and to listen to the gospel of reconciliation. It is a place for reflection and taking stock; it provides refuge and encouragement. It offers a vital emotional and spiritual space, inviting us to confront those questions which are so easily forgotten in the stress and strain of everyday life.

Forty voluntary church guides are on hand to show visitors through the building and to present faith and the church through sight, speech, and hearing. In addition, trained counsellors are on hand for visitors seeking answers and advice.

The daily prayer services at noon and in the evenings are oases in our everyday lives. Following the ringing of the Peace Bell, the Frauenkirche invites people to take part in the noon prayer and to listen to the »queen of instruments«. At 6 PM the day finishes with the evening prayer. These services are each followed by a central church tour.

Church music is a major component of all services. The choirs of the Frauenkirche perform at the Sunday worship service at 11 AM. A cantata is performed at the main worship service once a month and on church holidays.

Instrumental church music can be heard during the evening worship services at 6 PM. These evening services receive their special character through thematic sermon cycles.

58 Church Service.

Religious Sunday music, organ vespers, and the organ concert series underscore the particular importance of religious music in the Frauenkirche.

The Saturday evening concerts continue a long musical tradition in the Frauenkirche. Programme planning is made in recognition of the high demands which a musically refined public justifiably places upon us. The great masses and oratorios are just as strongly represented in the concert programme as are works promoting the idea of peace and understanding between peoples.

The newly reconstructed Frauenkirche displays both the wounds of war and the possibilities for healing and a new beginning which God grants to us despite our human failings, committing us to work for a reconciliation which extends beyond all borders.

The idea of peace and reconciliation is the common theme of all activities at the Frauenkirche. It stands for the commitment, arising from our remembrance of the victims and destruction of war, to work toward the co-operation and reconciliation of nations, denominations, and cultures.

To be sure, memory cannot isolate the fate of Dresden from the aggressive and murderous war unleashed by Germany seven years before the destruction of our city, nor can it ignore the fact

59 As a place of encounter the Frauenkirche regularly hosts panel discussions.

that only a few years previously the synagogues of this country were burned and the Jews were disenfranchised, plundered, and ultimately exterminated. Those who wish to learn from the history of the Frauenkirche must also ponder man's susceptibility to inhuman ideologies.

Conscious commemoration thus becomes the starting point and rallying point for endeavours aimed at the present and future well-being of humankind.

Commemoration, reconciliation, and striving for a humane and peaceful world occur not only in individual events such as lectures and youth encounters, but also form the basis and essence of the Frauenkirche's day-to-day operations.

It is also essential to pick up on the questions underlying current social conflicts and to let the voice of the church ring out loud and clear. The podium discussions are there to address this concern.

60 Inspecting the construction in a boom lift.

YOU ARE OUR ROCK!

The Frauenkirche has reclaimed its place at the heart of the city and gets across its message of peace and reconciliation to people from all over the world every day. It is the overwhelming commitment of many thousands of donors which made the rebuilding of the Frauenkirche possible. To maintain the church for future generations, a great deal of civic support will continue to be required in future.

Keeping the Frauenkirche open day by day for the numerous, varied events held there runs up costs for power, water and district heating, ongoing maintenance costs and cleaning which amount to roughly one million euros per annum. Every year, the Frauenkirche closes for six days in January for repairs. The investment which will be needed to maintain the church over the coming decades is constantly rising.

Every donation helps! For a donation at € 300 or more you can symbolically adopt a stone in the Frauenkirche. The symbolic adoption of a seat is possible for a donation of € 2,500 or more.

More than 1,000 seats have already been »adopted« and brass plaques with donors' names can still be affixed to another 600 seats. As well as a donation or contribution to the endowment fund during your lifetime it is also possible to help maintain the Frauenkirche in Dresden by making a provision in your will.

The Frauenkirche Foundation Dresden is responsible for maintaining the church building and shaping life in the Frauenkirche based on a 99-year leasehold. The Frauenkirche Foundation Dresden mainly raises funds for these tasks from donations.

Your donation will help achieve the aims of the foundation's work.

Thank you very much!

AT A GLANCE

Church services
All visitors are invited to attend church services, which are open to all.
On Sundays and public holidays: 11 a.m. with a choir and 6 p.m. with instrumental church music; an Anglican service is held on one Sunday a month at 6 p.m. in English.

Devotions with organ music and a central guided tour of the church
Find peace at morning and evening worship. Afterwards, a church guide holds a presentation from the pulpit on the history, architecture and iconography of the church.
Monday – Saturday 12 noon
Monday – Wednesday and on Friday 6 p.m.

Ecumenical evening prayer
Thursday 6 p.m. in the lower church

Open Door
During »Open Door« times, visitors are invited to come in and explore the main church and crypt.
Monday – Friday, usually 10 – 12 a.m. and 1 – 6 p.m. Times may change or be reduced at the weekend due to rehearsals.

Guided tours
For tours of the galleries, please ask on the day. Devotions are followed by a central guided tour of the church. During »Open Door« times guides answer questions. Group bookings can be made for devotions, followed by a general tour of the church, or for audioguide tours, guided tours of the galleries and tours of the dome.
Audio-guides can be hired during »Open Door« times in six languages.

61 Silhouette of the Old Town: View from the Neustädter bank.

Film »The Fascination of the Frauenkirche«

The film »The Fascination of the Frauenkirche« covers the history and reconstruction of the Frauenkirche, and life in the church.

Film showing: »The Fascination of the Frauenkirche«; Length: approx. 25 minutes, in the lower level of the Frauenkirche during »Open Door« times

Music

Music is provided by ensembles and choirs which are popular all over the world, plus the Frauenkirche's own ensemble and choirs, directed by cantor Matthias Grünert with the Frauenkirche's own organist Samuel Kummer or guest organists at the Kern organ.

Concerts: Saturdays at 8 p.m., fortnightly Sunday music at 3 p.m., organ music on Wednesdays at 8 p.m. alternating with the organs in the city center of Dresden.

Dome visits

On their way up to the Frauenkirche's 67-metre-high viewing platform, visitors find out about the unique architecture of the most important stone-domed building north of the Alps. From the top they have a panoramic view across Dresden and its surroundings.

Opening times March to October: Monday – Saturday 10 a.m. – 6 p.m. | Sunday 12.30 – 6 p.m.; November to February: Monday – Saturday 10 a.m. – 4 p.m. | Sunday 12.30 – 4 p.m. Please note the entry requirements!

Exhibition

Exhibition room in honour of those who have donated to, supported and taken part in reconstruction and maintenance, in the lower level of the Frauenkirche during »Open Door« times

62 10th anniversary of the consecration of the Frauenkirche – Jubilee concert, October 2015.

SERVICE
Frauenkirche Dresden Foundation
Georg-Treu-Platz 3 | 01067 Dresden
phone +49 (0)351.65606-100
fax +49 (0)351.65606-112
stiftung@frauenkirche-dresden.de

Pastor's office
phone +49 (0)351.65606-510
fax +49 (0)351.65606-520
pfarrbuero@frauenkirche-dresden.de

Guided tours
phone +49 (0)351.65606-100
fax +49 (0)351.65606-108
fuehrungen@frauenkirche-dresden.de

Ticket service
phone +49 (0)351.65606-701
fax +49 (0)351.65606-108
ticket@frauenkirche-dresden.de

Visitor centre & Ticket service
Georg-Treu-Platz 3 (1st floor) | 01067 Dresden
Monday – Friday 9 a.m. – 6 p.m., Saturday
9 a.m. – 12 a.m.

Donations
phone +49 (0)351.65606-225
fax +49 (0)351.65606-211
spenden@frauenkirche-dresden.de

Donations account
Commerzbank AG
IBAN: DE60 8508 0000 0459 4885 00
BIC: DRESDEFF850

EVENTS AND DATES

11th century	A chapel is constructed on the site of the modern-day Frauenkirche.
1722	The Dresden town council commissions master carpenter George Bähr to design a new structure.
1726	Cornerstone laid on 26 August.
1734	The Frauenkirche is consecrated on 28 February – still incomplete without an organ and with a temporary altar.
1736	Completion of the 12,000 t stone dome.
1738	George Bähr dies on 16 March.
1743	The Frauenkirche is completed with the installation of the gilded tower cross on 27 May.
	1812/1813 The Frauenkirche is misused as a warehouse and supply depot for the army during the siege by Emperor Napoleon I.
1885	Erection of the Luther monument in front of the Frauenkirche: the head was fashioned by Ernst August Rietschel (1804–1861), the body by Adolf von Donndorf (1835–1916).
1938–1942	Comprehensive protection measures are carried out under the direction of the architects Arno Kiesling and Prof. Georg Rüth.
1945	On the morning of 15 February – two days following the disastrous bombing of Dresden – the Frauenkirche's gutted central dome collapses.
after 1945	No funds are available for the reconstruction. The ruin of the Frauenkirche is left as a memorial.
1982	On 13 February participants in the Ecumenical Peace Forum in the Kreuzkirche march to the ruin of the Frauenkirche with candles. They stage a vigil, sing, and pray through the night for world peace.
Reconstruction	One year after the end of the war, the Evangelical-Lutheran State Church of Saxony made a request for donations to rebuild the church. The State Office for Historical Preservation conducted the first studies on the possibility of an archaeological reconstruction. However, political conditions do not permit the continuation of the initial efforts. In the late 1980s, leading politicians from the Federal Republic called for the reconstruction

	of the Frauenkirche and began collecting donations. At the time of the »Wende« in 1989, a local Dresden citizens group formed with the goal of rebuilding the church.
1990	On 13 February the Call from Dresden was issued to the world for help in rebuilding the Frauenkirche.
1992	The Dresden Frauenkirche Foundation is founded as an association.
1993	The archaeological rubble clearing begins on 4 January. On 1 June the old tower cross is discovered among the debris.
1994	The Frauenkirche Foundation is approved as a non-profit foundation in August. With the laying of the first stone on 27 May, the archaeological reconstruction begins.
1995	Erection of the external structure, a new edifice which surrounds the Lower Church like a horseshoe over an area of 1,300 m^2 and houses the utility areas required for a modern building.
1996	Consecration of the Lower Church on 21 August.
2000	On February 13, his Royal Highness, the Duke of Kent, presents the new tower cross to the Frauenkirche Foundation – a gift from the British people.
2003	On 23 May the capstone of the upper pressure ring of the main dome is laid. On 4 May the seven new bells of the Frauenkirche are festively consecrated. The new chimes ring out for the first time on Pentecost (7 June).
2004	The removal of all scaffolding on 19 July represents the external completion of the reconstruction.
2005	On 13 February, the Frauenkirche Foundation becomes a member of the International Society of the Cross of Nails.
30 Oct. 2005	Consecration of the Dresden Frauenkirche.